Book 1

Day Trading

A beginner trading guide

Book 2

Dividend investing

A quick beginner guide

Book 3

Penny Stock

A quick Beginner guide

All this book

By Richard Smiths

Book 1

Day Trading

A beginner trading guide

By Richard Smiths

Table of Contents

Introduction

I want to thank you and congratulate you for downloading the book, Day Trading. This book contains proven steps and strategies on how to earn money in Day Trading. I am truly convinced that I am able to provide you with the value and information that you are looking for.

In this eBook, I am going to present you all the information you need to possess if you plan to get into this business. My focus will be on showing you what are the day trading basics, as well as all the things you definitely need to know before you get into this business.

There are so many trading books out there on the market that is simply made up of ideas that can be easily found on the Internet for free, and this book is not one of them. This book is not another "Day Trading for

Dummies" type of book but contains real strategies and solid school of thoughts of accomplished day traders. It is a no-nonsense, honest guide to successful day trading that I believe anyone can learn from.

Day trading can definitely be simple, but please, do not make the mistake of thinking it is easy. It is very far from that.

I know that you probably heard many people saying "Day trading is easy" and I know you saw plenty of websites telling you how you can achieve success in day trading after reading a couple of pages or attending some stupid online class. I would definitely like if this was true and that, magically, you can become a successful trader overnight.

Please, do not be fooled with this. Like in every profession on the world, you are going to need much more than attending a class or reading an eBook in order to become a master at something. You need a solid education, a good plan and some experience.

You will get exact and reliable information in regards to the topic and issue covered. The book is sold with the information that the publisher is not necessary to render accounting, officially acceptable, or otherwise, professional services. If information is necessary, legal or acceptable, an experienced individual in the profession should be ordered.

Thanks again for downloading this book, I hope you enjoy it!

This document is geared towards providing exact and reliable information in regards to the topic and issue covered. The publication is sold with the idea that the publisher is not required to render accounting, officially permitted, or otherwise, qualified services. If advice is necessary, legal or professional, a practiced individual in the profession should be ordered.

- From a Declaration of Principles which was accepted and approved equally by a Committee of the American Bar Association and a Committee of Publishers and Associations.

The information provided herein is stated to be truthful and consistent, in that any liability, in terms of inattention or otherwise, by any usage or abuse of any policies, processes, or directions contained within is

Chapter 1   What is Day trading ?

Day trading is defined as "the buying and selling of securities on the SAME day". It is usually done online and in hopes of taking advantage of and reaping benefits from small, short-term price fluctuations.

Here is an example: You could buy 1000 shares of Amazon stocks at 10:15 AM at let's say - $425 per share. 10 minutes later it rises to $426, you made $1 per share. Since you have bought 1000 shares, you just earned yourself $1000 in profit (minus a small commission for the brokerage). This potential to make that kind of money in such a short period of time is what attracts people to day trading. It is not uncommon to make $300 in 30 minutes, $600 in 20 minutes, or $1500 in 5 minutes, and so on.

it is not always this simple. I know plenty of people and websites are selling you the idea that you can get rich overnight by trading stocks. It's not necessarily impossible, but it's rather unrealistic.

However, you can make a lot of money if you possess certain tools and know special strategies. As with any profession, if you want success, you need a PLAN! Without a plan, you are wasting time, and even worse, you are wasting money.

I will try to show you all the mistakes you need to avoid, as well as some of my best strategies that can be useful. If you are determined and committed, I am convinced you can accomplish anything you put your mind on.

However, day trading is not for everyone. If you are not good at facing losses, I recommend you NOT to go into this field of business.

The cold hard truth is: over 90% of traders make a loss in trading. Many of them gave up before they give themselves the chance to make a profit.

Why do most day traders fail?

That is a common question for a people, so quite a few came and thus many was unable. The staggering percentage folks who failed presented rise for the opinion of which trading can be mysterious, as well as even a tremendous scam of which profits just the loaded and effective.

Now, there are many reasons the reason people fail with this business. The 2 major main reasons why day traders lose money consistently could be because of their lack of knowledge in regards to the notion regarding "risk vs reward" along with their lack of discipline. A trader can enter a trade wanting to make $1 per share, however if his or her potential risk is $2, it's not necessarily worth using the buy and sell. Many usually are so blinded through the reward that they can fail to produce a well-formed strategy before getting in. This kind of, in convert, leads for the second cause, which can be discipline. I firmly think that the math concepts of trading is extremely straightforward along with easy. It is a person's emotion that always screws the game. Being unsure of when in order to cut burning, being stubborn on the losing buy and sell and revenge trading the stock they have got just shed money about are a few examples regarding ill-disciplined trading. These dealers ultimately fail and maybe they are not who you wish to be.

Many people have shed their personal savings on stock investing and for that reason, trading can often be seen for evil. Day trading investing is often synonymous having gambling along with betting, but in the event you take time to learn along with appreciate the marketplace, you will realize that day trading is vastly different from your standard gambling.

Chapter 2   Why you should start day trading

Here are some reasons why I believe day trading is the actual path to wealth.

One, the money. That's obvious; I mean that's probably why you are reading this book in the first place.

Two, location independence: you can do day trading anywhere in the world where there is an internet connection. If you choose to sit at home, at a café, or at the pool or beach (as long as there is Wi-Fi), you're good.

Three, you can make your own hours. If you choose to work just one hour a day, that's fine. If you want to work less or more, that's fine, too. Whatever works for you?

Four, your race does not matter, your looks do not matter, and your social status does not matter. You also don't need a college degree, even though knowledge or an economic background obviously doesn't hurt, but no expensive 4-year degree or more is required. None of these things are important. You only need to have sufficient funds to trade.

Other than that, there are so many differences between day trading and all the other businesses. You do not have to hire anyone; you do not have to have employees and manage your business, you do not have to worry about their performances etc.. You do not have to rent office space or to worry about customers, invoices, equipment.

These are all the reasons why day trading should be your next big thing. If you are motivated and determined, then there is no excuse not to start earning money with day trading even today. Later in this eBook, I will show you some of the possible earning as well, which will motivate you even more. Anyway, let's stick to the basics for now.

The following are some of the major reasons why you should start day trading:

1) Reduced capital investment

Like a most businesses, you don't need lots of money to start day trading investing. In the

United states, you need almost $1000 to start day trading investing in the foreign currency market and just regarding $25, 000 to get started on day trading throughout stocks. This is somewhat amount money considering the leverage you get and the amount of profits you can rip from your trading.

2) The particular Returns are quick

If you want a profitable business with instantaneous benefits, then day exchanging is that business. In day exchanging, you buy and also sell financial instruments on the same day. This simply means that you begin counting your profits some hours or even units after entering a new trade. You may also convert your profits into cash promptly. You can reinvest your wages and make far more profits. This makes this a wonderful business for someone who would like to make money more quickly.

3) No need to hire worker

If what can be keeping you from starting a profitable business is the stress of suffering employees then day trading investing is list of positive actions. In day exchanging, you don't need to hire employees that you can comfortably do it on your own. All you need is usually a trading account, a few devices and your ventures.

4) It costs less to own

The total cost of accomplishing day trading is quite minimal. Other than your investment all other things you need are much less expensive costly than running the original business. The commission per trade is quite minimal and sometimes you will need to pay less than $10. You don't need an place of work, inventory, and machinery which often further reduces the price tag on starting and running your work time trading business. Other issues that is included in traditional office business including insurance, goods shipping and delivery and handling, displays and promotions and others don't apply. The fact that you don't handle customers directly means that you don't ought to spend more in running your work day trading business. Furthermore, you save considerable time as you don't ought to handle invoices, companies and customer products and services activities.

5) It gives equal opportunity for earning

Unlike a normal day job where there's discrepancies in earning depending on educational background, career title, race and in some cases gender, there isn't such a part of day trading. All you want to earn is usually a solid plan and also good judgment. If you have for a while been thinking involving economic activity to undertake that doesn't come with the usual discrimination issues in the day job, then consider day trading investing. Sometimes you can be discriminated against depending on your color as well as past history from the traditional business or when searching for work. There isn't such discrimination in day trading investing.

6) It put in at home to learn and also manage

Day trading is usually a simple art to know. All you need to learn is the standard. Once you grasp them, you can start trading. Since all you could do in a new trade is keep an eye on the entry along with the exit, day trading is quite easy to learn and manage. And can truly take you just a couple of hours each day for making lots of profits.

Chapter 3   How to get started

To many people new professionals, these are the most important issues. "What should it take to get started? What broker must i choose? Must i need any supercomputer? " My partner and i don't feel that answers to any of these issues will assist you to become a successful trader overnight.

If an individual ever considered getting into ecommerce, then I'm able to guess you might have strong motivation and definately will to come to be rich. As you know, being motivated being rich is actually saying, "You are already ". On the other hand, you do not desire to be rich, rely on me. You would like to be wealthy!

As many individuals are not aware of the variation between "rich" as well as "wealthy", Let me show you the principle difference.

•   Being rich" means you might have fortune (which doesn't mean you might have earned them).

• "Being wealthy" indicates that you've time to savor money you might have earned and time for it to do what for you to do.

In my opinion, there usually are three strategies to become wealthy:

• Start your own personal company or your own personal internet small business

• Invest into real-estate

• Start a profession in trading!

Obviously, the very first two usually are much harder and much more complicated. I am going to explain an individual why. To get started on your very own company and possess a profitable online business, you are going to need to make your very own product, market place your product or service, find clients, sell these individuals your product or service, and for the end, accumulate the payments.

Successful trading stems from good habits and discipline, and they are not skills that you can acquire in a short time of moment. With that said, you do have to spend some time thinking about how much you are prepared to risk as well as which brokers are made for you to help you trade of your means as well as without too much stress.

How Much Money Do I Need To Start?

I hope you might be interested to find about how much cash you actually want to get started in order to day business.

Unfortunately for many that actually want to participate inside high regular trading, there is something called the 25k rule in the usa. This rule states you need to maintain no less than at the very least $25, 000 within your account constantly. This will be the minimum amount the SEC requires proper who wants to make 4 and up trades for each 5 morning period. That means once your account balance would drop because of $24, 999, the rule kicks in therefore you would only be permitted to trade 3 x per 5 morning period, which in turn obviously prevents you through actual day trading. So retain this planned.

You have to know that there exists emotion involved during trading that may never end up being fully experienced by simply paper exchanging. In various other words, you may not take papers trading severely because no real money is involved. Before you put in place any number of real cash, always select the thought preparation that you can lose the whole thing. I realize that this could be difficult to understand just through words, because a person actually dealing with it. I generally recommend people to print or take note of their principles of trading using a Post-It and place it on your keyboard where you can see the item during exchanging. This can always serve as being a reminder to keep your awesome during exchanging hours and not bust your account in a moment connected with folly.

Equipment: What Is Needed In Order To Trade Successfully?

Hmm, let's see. Oh, how can I forget that? You are probably willing to know what else, except money, you are going to need if you decide to get into this business.

Well, here is a short list and I am going to devote couple of paragraphs for each one of them.

1. A computer

2. An internet connection

3. A broker

4. Good strategy

5. Charting software

As you can see, these are five must haves for this business. You will never achieve success in day trading if you miss some of these.

When talking about a computer, I wanted you to let you know that you do not need the latest technology. Most of the charting software is compatible with old technology and they always work perfectly on Windows (my recommendation) so I advise you not to spend big amounts of money. What I would do is I would purchase a second screen so you can have charting software on one screen and trading platform on the second one.

Reliable internet connection is must. Never cheapen here.

BROKERS

When you would like a dealer, you have to find the one that serves the needs you have.

Understand in which brokers won't make or even break your trading; it is yourself in which dictates this specific. However, a great broker will make your lifestyle easier and let you be more centered on the day trading as an alternative to worrying about stuffs that are significantly less important.

In other words, a beneficial broker is the one that complements your trading technique. If you get you have greater success stock trading on your short part, you desire to find brokers which have good borrows regarding shares to short, permitting you to short a greater variety involving stocks. You may determine your style of exchanging from activities in cardstock trading. If you prefer to trade large quantities (>10000) involving low-priced stocks, you would want to find a dealer that charges commission over a per business basis. A per share foundation commission will likely be way too costly for an individual. The key to the present is to discover the broker in which suits your style of trading probably the most. Personally, I also like broker agents with excellent customer satisfaction because often during the trading hrs, you need a response to problems fast and also a great broker customer satisfaction that will be easily reachable will go further in providing you a more pleasant trading experience with a lesser amount of headaches. This is the list involving brokers, i have personally used, before few a long time and my overview of them:

Sure Trader

Pros: No PDT rule, you can open an account for as little as $500.Allows international traders to day trade US stock markets. Decent shares to borrow. Low commission at $5 trade per 10000 shares.

Cons: Very poor customer service. Slow response time and poor grasp of English. They are also based in Bahamas and are therefore less transparent.

Recommendation: I will say if you are starting off with a small account and wish to avoid the PDT, this is your only option. Both their trading platform and customer service are hit and miss cases.

Center point Securities

Pros: Excellent customer service and wide ranges of shares available to short. They use Sterling Pro platform that is one of the best out there. Overall, a very high quality product.

Cons: You will require at least $50,000 to open an account.

Recommendation: I highly recommend Center point Securities IF you are thinking about going in fulltime with more than $50,000 to spare and already have some experience in trading.

Interactive Broker

Pros: 2 tiers of structure that caters to both frequency traders and high volume traders. Has one of the lowest commissions in the industry. Very wide range of investment vehicles.

Cons: $10,000 initial sum required. Sub-par customer service. Average borrow list.

Recommendation: IB is a decent broker from my experience. But lately, I have not been trading on it unless I need to locate more shares to short.

Speed Trader

Pros: 10,000 symbol short list and has good locates for stocks you want to short. $0.001 per share in commission. ECN fee rebates.

Cons: Mobile trading only available to iOS products.

Recommendation: I will recommend Speed Trader because of their highly negotiable commission structure which may allow a trader to pay as low as $1 per trade as well as their robust shares to short list.

Charting software

It is also necessary, of course. I am not going to spend too many words on this. There is a lot of quality information on the Internet, which can give you a review of all charting software and provide you with all the features.

Last but not least, a trading strategy. You can have the best computer, best internet connection, most experienced broker, best software and an account with huge balance, but if you do not have a trading strategy, you are only going to lose money. So, you should be aware all of this trading strategy.

Fancy Trading Terms Simplified

So before we get into more detail talking about stocks, forex, etc. let's look at a couple of essential terms that you will hear pretty much all the time when getting into day trading or stock investing in general.

Capital requirements pretty much refers to how much money you need in order to invest. Your capital investment will vary depending on if you are using stocks, options or futures. Options, for example, are cheaper than stocks but carry more value (but also more risk).

Leverage is basically how much benefit you receive out of something in relation to how much you initially put in. For example, while you can make a lot of money off of futures, you actually don't have to put in or spend that much when buying them. High leverage is awesome but also usually means the possibility of losing a lot, it all and sometimes even more than you have.

Volatility basically means fluctuation. If one says, "the market is very volatile right now", it means there are a lot changes in price movement in a short period of time, in other words, lots of ups and downs at this moment. This is usually good for us day traders since we can take advantage of this situation as prices fluctuate.

Liquidity refers to the degree of availability of an asset. Cash, for example, is highly liquid while real estate is not. You can trade cash immediately, while it takes a while until you actually sell (liquidate) a property.

Then there are also the two essential terms "going long" as well as "going short".

Going "long" means buying and speculating that the price of something will go up. This is your standard trade. You buy a stock for $50 and hope it will go up to $60, once it gets up to $60, you sell it. You took a "long" position.

However, when you go "short", you actually bet against that stock. You are speculating that this particular stock will decrease in value. Professional traders often use this strategy when they feel like a stock cannot rise more than it has already done. The concept is easy in essence and much benefit can be derived from this when one has enough experience. Going short can be awesome but you can also shoot yourself in the foot with this.

Chapter 4 Building a Watch list

Carrying out homework is important to per day trader. A smart trader the moment related learning how to trade to help taking examinations in college. He used to take any statistics course in school and it also was a few days before the ultimate paper. Everybody was permitted to bring within the A4 sized piece of paper to write all your formulae or comments about it and bring into the exam area. It was such as a cheat page of sorts. He didn't organize the quiz but he squeezed hold of any photocopied version with the cheat sheet with the smartest college student in course. Armed your genius good article, he went directly into take your exam. But in the exam, he can't do a single question. He didn't produce the be unfaithful sheet, and he or she didn't learn how to use it at all. He didn't learn how to apply any formula as well as spent quite a while just to get where an item of information was written. He didn't go through the process connected with understanding why certain things were prepared down as well as certain things weren't. Only the person who personally wrote it will understand and they're the style of people who flourish in your exam. The identical logic relates to trading. If you only blindly make use of somebody's strategies watching lists as well as hope you can replicate his or her success, you will be in to get a rude shock in the actual investing. You must understand the rationale behind just about every move as well as ultimately, you wish to create your own plan that works by yourself. In this particular chapter, I can explain on ways to form ones watch record and with any luck ,, you can understand some of the thought method that passes through my head when i find stocks and options to industry.

Every day, you need to enter this market with any clean slate and a well-formed approach. The best time and energy to formulate this course of action is accomplishing research within the night before. The marketplace closes from the afternoon therefore you always expand the pattern of getting an hour or so at night to review your trades during the day. This means that you can get better and better over time.

A excellent portion of times should also be used to creating your watch list. A watch list contains a listing of stock that you just will probably want to play tomorrow depending on your screening criteria. Usually, you create a listing of not greater than 10 stocks on the list the night before. Next morning prior to market unwraps, you will have to review this particular list as well as update it in line with the pre-market action with the stocks. you possibly can either sign up for those which can be not trading as outlined by your approach or add more tickers who're setting up nicely through pre-market.

If you would like to trade NASDAQ listed stocks and selective NYSE stocks; you hardly ever touch OTCBB or pink sheet stocks due to the lack of volume and liquidity. You can trade using the one-minute candlestick chart and do not use any fancy indicators such as the MACD or the RSI. It is my philosophy to keep things clear and easy. NASDAQ provides the greatest liquidity and you can move in and out of the market relatively easy. To the surprise of many, you like to keep your stock screening process really,

REALLY simple. You can use 4 main indicators to determine if a stock can be traded.

1) Volume

2) Range

3) Support/Resistance

4) Chart Pattern

VOLUME

I look for charts that are in play with tons of volume. You want a large audience to be following the chart, because this way, support and resistance lines will become a self-fulfilling prophecy. Typically, a chart should have at least 1,000,000 daily shares traded for me to consider it. The volume should also have seen a spike in comparison with the past daily volume of the stock.

RANGE

The next criteria is range, I look for a stock that has at least 0.25 cents in range. Anything less than that is not worth the time because of how little the stock moves every day. Penny stocks are a different matter because of their low stock price. A large range indicates to a trader that it is volatile and he can make a larger amount of money per share traded.

SUPPORT AND RESISTANCE

With regards to using complex analysis, I really do not more than complicate matters. You probably have learnt coming from other buying and selling books about using fancy indicators including moving averages as well as Donchian routes. I don't use these. The simply indicators you may use for stock investing are service and level of resistance lines. If you locate that particular indicators are most often working well in your case already, then that is great. Stick with the information you are aware of and what may seem to work by yourself.

Support along with resistance lines have become important to determine if the stock can be traded. If your stock tries go higher and pauses past an argument of level of resistance, there might be a surge with volume due to the fact everybody believes the stock could surge that is certainly when this stock starts to pattern upwards. Nonetheless, it is not always the way it is. There can be cases associated with fake outbreaks or breakdowns that capture people into convinced that the investment can trend within the anticipated path. Eventually, in the event the stock chart won't move not surprisingly, these men and women panic along with the stock may well spike within the opposite path. It is essential to get a plan in the event they occur. Once the breakout on a long information happened, I like to buy on the pull returning or because the chart dips.

Entries have become important into a day trader when just about every tick matters. I don't choose to chase the stock if it's at the highs when you never know when a chart may possibly pull returning and freeze. Even though, eventually, it may possibly rise back and you will be accurate, you save the throbbing headache of seeing the information going against you.

HOW TO USE THE WATCHLIST

The Watch list is created so that you can have a better feel of the momentum of the stocks you want to trade on the next day. If you already have a Watchlist written out, you save yourself the panic of looking through a whole list of stocks again. In the next morning after you have compiled your Watchlist, you want to be looking at these stocks and look out for a confirmation of your trade idea. Is the stock moving in the direction as you anticipated it to be? Is a trend forming in your desired direction? If the stock is not moving how you think it should be, take it off your immediate Watchlist at market open and allow the stock to set up throughout the trading day first. This way, you are actually narrowing down your Watchlist to a few stocks that you are most confident about playing at the market open.

Chapter 5 The risk and potential

At first need to create a plan. A plan will inform you when exactly you need to stop your trade to cut losses or help to increase a situation. When you need to exit a new trade to now you should profit or maybe size down on a position. As with each industry, you always aim for a advantageous risk or reward rate of at the least 3: 1. Risk or reward ratio is usually determined through support and resistance outlines. It means that if people enter a new trade using a stock price tag of $6 and you also are able to risk a lack of $1, you should be sure the chart is placed up for any potential pay back of $3. This is a simple rule of thumb which My spouse and i govern every one of my trading.

Cutting loss

Cutting losses has become one of my major rules once i day industry. A great deal of traders won't cut losses simply because BELIEVE how the stock will rebound. When you are trading, never allow yourself to lose greater than you earn, and to do that, you should cut ones losses decisively. You possibly can always enter this market again once the chart set itself upwards, but you'll be able to never get back the money you might have just missing.

How to find out a strong resistance or perhaps support collection?

A solid support or maybe resistance collection is one which has been tested with the chart more often than not but by no means been productively broken away from. A strong distinctive line of support or maybe resistance usually gives a better and more accurate determine for risk or pay back because when the information goes near this collection, the group believes how the line will serve for the reason that support or maybe resistance once more and reply accordingly. This becomes an incredibly strong self-fulfilling prediction. It is also useful to note that in the event the chart breaks away from a strong distinctive line of support or maybe resistance, it will typically experience a strong move towards its large.

When exchanging a inventory, it is significant to check out both your daily and intraday chart to spot if a real line exists within the 3-6month moment frames. In the event it prevails, you need to respect that strong distinctive line of support/resistance while trading your intraday information and plan your risk versus pay back accordingly.

COMPLETE NUMBER PSYCHOLOGY

Paying focus on whole range marks in addition helps inside gauging danger versus reward for any trade. Many traders focus on whole greenback marks ($10. 00) or maybe half greenback marks ($10. 50) a lot more closely. One example is, if your stock currently is priced from $9. 64 intraday and trending larger, many professionals will believe that it can easily push to $10. 00 and purchase into this. Once your stock visits $10. 00, everybody are going to be thinking of taking earnings and market off. At this time, the $10. 00 level is acting as a psychological distinctive line of resistance. It is usually wise to focus on this full and 50 % dollar mark if you are trading and make ideas based down these numbers.

Chapter 6   Advice for day trading

In the last chapter of the eBook, I am going to provide you some of the advice for day trading success, which you may not know. They are equally important as every other information in this eBook because you need to avoid some of the mistakes I am going to point out as well as concentrate on some good things and facts I am going to mention in the next couple of paragraphs.

I would like this chapter to be about pointing you out the mistakes you can make in day trading that could keep you away from success and profit.

I believe I found seven big mistakes any day trader can make. I found this to be extremely useful because if you remember, I mentioned that only 1 out of 10 people who try to make money with day trading actually succeed. Do you know what does that actually mean? Your chances to fail are much bigger than to succeed.

Here, you can see 7 advices for a successful day trading.

1: Do not Over-analyzing

The problem people usually make in day trading is that they over-analyze the market to find a trend. This approach is often very wrong and there is a misconception among people that says "more complicated formula and algorithm you have, the better are the odds for making profit." That is simply not true. Yes, it is good to have a formula and algorithm you follow, but you cannot forget one of the most important rules in day trading. You buy when the market is going up and sell when the market is going down

2: Be patient to take your profits

Do you know why only 1 out of 10 people reach success in day trading? It is because 9 out of 10 people are greedy. I do not know how many times I mentioned this and I am not sure how many times I will say it again; Day trading success comes from consistency and taking small profits. It is not a get-rich-quick scheme and success is possible only if you are patient.

3: Know the limit of losses

If you recall, I have already mentioned that if you want to reach success in day trading, you need to be okay with losing money. That is not strange, not even to most successful day traders. They lose money, too. A lot! But they are successful because they know how to limit their losses.

It is of extreme importance to know when to exit a certain trade to save money. It is always better to lose $300 than $3000 because you stayed to long.

4: Sticking with the right market

I am sure that you are going to reach success with certain type of market. The question is whether you will tie yourself to the same market forever. You need to follow the market! YOU NEED TO BE THE MARKET!

Another important fact is that you need to be in the market that is moving because, as I repeatedly say, buy when the market goes up and sell when it goes down. From that, we can conclude that you need to be okay with changes and adapting on new markets constantly. Go where the money is, and money is never in the steady market.

5: Develop a trading strategy

If you think you can succeed in today's world, in any profession, without a plan and a strategy, you are terribly wrong. No one can do that. That is the reason why I devoted a whole chapter to writing a successful trading strategy and its importance.

6: Control over yourself

When people describe me, they usually say that I am an incredibly calm person. This is because I learned how to control my emotions and my thoughts because if you do not control thoughts, they will control you.

Calmness should be the main characteristic of every successful trader. If you do not how to control your greediness, your fear or your panic, you will never succeed.

7: Do not Overtrading

Finally yet importantly, learn when it is enough. I think I talked about this on every seminar I had about day trading. Overtrading is the common problem of every day trader. When you reach your weekly goals, just stop! There is no reason to keep trading if you already made the profit you want.

People usually make these seven mistakes. I know you need to avoid them if you want profit. Now I am going to list some of the characteristics of successful day traders. Pay attention if you want to develop some serious skills.

They do not blame other people because of their losses and failures. They think that is normal and there is no reason to blame your broker or any other person because you lost money on certain trade.

They have a system. In the system, they developed every possible situation that can happen. They do not stay in the losing trade and they do not hurry and rush into trades. They are precise, they take their time and they are well aware of each step they make. That is why they are successful.

They learned how to adapt. Maybe I didn't stress out how this is important in day trading because market constantly changes and if you want to keep having profits, you need to go with the change.

Conclusion

I hope this book was able to help you to understand about how to day trade.

I hope you absorbed all the information in this eBook because you are going to need it. I am sure you are going to remember the most important facts because I was pointing them out constantly. You may not know how they are important now, but you will definitely remember what I was saying once when you start trading.

Thank you and good luck!

Book 2

Dividend Investing

A beginner trading guide

By Richard Smiths

Table of Contents

Introduction

I want to thank you and congratulate you for downloading the book, Dividend investing.

This book contains proven steps and strategies on how to get started quickly on the path of dividend investing and ready to hit the ground running.

Dividend Investing is an investing approach where money is invested in stocks, bonds, mutual funds for seeking dividends that are regularly distributed to invest in the form of either cash or extra shares. Dividend Investing has over the time served investing community very well thru various up or down market cycles with lesser risk and helped investors accumulate wealth over a period of time.

There is no easier way to achieve financial independence than to make more money while spending less. This principle has held true for generations and will continue to do so for years to come. What you do with the money you save is even more pivotal. Savvy individuals choose to invest it. Understanding different avenues of investing is pivotal to ensure your success in personal finance and towards your retirement.

If you are a beginner, be a young kid on the block, young or middle eage or retiring women or man, and want to learn how to start dividend investing, this book is for you and will guide you with step by step instructions in easy to understand language without too much gibberish and hold your hand while you start your happy journey towards building a rich dividend portfolio. It's never too early or too late to begin this path,but you need to start now for your own rich life to enjoy.

You will get exact and reliable information in regards to the topic and issue covered. The book is sold with the information that the publisher is not necessary to render accounting, officially acceptable, or otherwise, professional services. If information is necessary, legal or acceptable, an experienced individual in the profession should be ordered.

Thanks again for downloading this book, I hope you enjoy it!

Chapter 1   What is Dividend Investing

The dividend investing is considered one of the best ways for investors to collect steady and consistent returns.There are several people who invest in these dividend stocks to take advantage of that dependability before utilizing some of those incoming funds to invest back into more shares of stocks – kind of like playing with some house money after winning a few rounds of blackjack at the casino.

Dividend investing is seen as one of the strategy that has become a savior in this economic environment by providing dividends thru rain or shine. Power of dividends coupled with the compounding effect can produce hefty gains without taking too much risk and Ponzi schemes.

Many studies have found the effectiveness of dividends investing over a period of time. In fact, dividend investing could potentially empower you with rule of 36, rather than rule of 72, where investments could double in half time, if properly applied.

In case of dividend portfolio, asset allocation and diversification using a right mix of stocks/ETFs/Funds is paramount. As with any portfolio, there will some risk elements, but, goal is to minimize them. With high rewards, come higher risks and therefore, goal is to achieve decent returns with less risk using dividend investing. Diversification of assets significantly determines the outcome of the portfolio success, not the timing of the market according to various pundits.

There are companies that pay consistently increasing dividends are usually considered financially balanced, generating a dependable return on investment on the distinct dividends. Stable companies generally feature any slipping stock prices to generate it less alarming to the shareholders in the overall market. Because of this, they can be considered less of a risk compared to the companies that don't sell out those dividends as well as, in turn, see more sharp good and bad in the value.

With a lower risk to the investors of these kind of dividend stocks, they might be a more beautiful option for various investors – the actual young bucks who're hoping to obtain more income over the long term and for those who are looking to produce their retirement pay for. There are even those already in retirement who utilize money from dividend investing to supply a regular earnings while they aren't doing the work.

Another reason the particular dividend stocks get built confidence among dividend investors will be the correlation between the actual share prices and also the yield of gains through the dividends. When 1 rises, the different flows. There's also the consideration to the power of compounding the investments – having the generated cash flow and putting them on the stocks which will continue to build an increasing number of.

In other text, the money you have generated from your earnings will generate additional earnings and also the generations of producing earnings will carry on and follow as an investor continues to reinvest for time. This process may hypothetically turn one penny right into a very large sum of cash after about every thirty days.

If you take that particular penny and carry on and double your account each day for 30 days and nights, you could see your hard earned money grow from a number of cents to a couple dollars. Ten us dollars becomes $20, which often becomes $40, then $80, $160, $320, $640, nearly thousands and gradually millions. Sure, there are many of things who have to happen, plus it requires a minor luck. But theoretically, it can happen – regardless of whether it's a tad unrealistic.

This isn't expressing that any investor can get to see their particular money grow when realize utilize dividend trading. But it shows that money can, as well as likely will, grow in a process that Albert Einstein when called the eighth wonder from the world.

Many who enter the entire world of dividend investing might find the eventual rise of their rate of return because they continue to reinvest your money that comes of their returns to purchase.

Let's say you have 100 shares of a stock that offer at $50 every share – an investment around $5, 000. During that first year, the organization offers a 3. 5 percent dividend, to provide an income involving $125.

If the investor continues to see dividend growths involving 5 percent annually, that's a $5, 000 initial investment will be valued at just greater than $11, 200 after about two decades. This is while using the assumption that there will be no change in the stock price and there exists the reinvestment mentioned earlier.

Now let's get that same organization pay a quarterly dividend as opposed to one that pays annually. That's $5, 000 investment can grow to a tad bit more than $11, 650 with the same two decades to get a gain of about 133 percent. With the process of compounding, a $50, 000 investment can become an $116, 500 sum after that same stretch of time during which you will find reinvestments into the actual dividend folder.

Chapter 2   What is dividend growth

Dividend growth is an important statistic for the investors. The stocks where have high dividend yields are frequently attracted by the investors.

But what is the more important rather than the current size of the dividend is the pace at which it has been shrinking.You can see, the Growing dividend is a sign of good stock, which is committed to its stockholders. It is also a sign of more dividend, raise to come.

To see if there have any problems, perhaps the stakeholder's needs to dig a little deeper into the company's financial Dividend Growth Rate, While a shrinking dividend or which is over-sized and it can be considered as a warning sign of problems with the company.

Dividend Growth Rate

As with promises a big dividend means the stock's value has recently downed. To make the dividend income more without an increase in the actual amount of dollar in the dividend.

You can see, the dividend growth amount is the average rate of growth and stock's dividend has experienced for a certain period of time.

Depending on who's doing the analysis, there are numerous time periods you can use. But the phrase used must produce a statistic to help determine the best thing about owning a stock option.

A one hundred-year typical dividend growth rate seriously isn't a very applicable statistic. However, a five-year typical dividend growth rate could be spot on.

With regards to dividend growth price, a stock using a long history associated with dividend payments is usually admirable and may make the stock more desirable. But a newer history of both equally dividend payments and increases is often a better indicator with the stock potential dividend payouts for the coming years.

In addition to, of course, awareness is always critical to investment success. So research your options and calculate some sort of stock's dividend growth rate before you make an investment.

Compound Annual Growth Rates (Cagrs)

When thinking about dividend growth rates over many years, it is proper and useful to do with compounding account, as opposed to a simple average growth rate. When looking at growth rate information, be sure to distinguish between growth information that uses compounding as well as growth data that could not do and so. The only way to make certain about this is to consider the actual every year figures (which may differ, and then calculate an example growth rate when using the formula for CAGRs. This formula is usually somewhat difficult to complete manually,so it is best to use a web site to compute CAGRs for you.

Problems With CAGRs

Compound annual growth in costs will reflect this compounded growth right from the start of a time frame to the end. Any variation in growth rate during this time will not be reflected in this particular measure. The CAGR would be the rate at that a dividend could have grown if this had grown with a steady rate. Since hardly just about any investment grows at the exact same rate each year, the CAGR might possibly be characterized as a great "imaginary" number. The true point is of which any variation within growth rate over a long time is definitely not reflected through the CAGR.

Dividend Growth Committing uses rolling five-year CAGRs over a reasonable length of time frames (preferably 20 years) to detect the two average CAGR as well as any variation within dividend growth rates through this period.

6 Advantages of Dividend Growth Investing

1. Allows an investor to get Get Paid to Wait

2. Dividend Growth Compounding

3. Take Advantage of Bear Markets

4. Capital Preservation

5. Create an Income Stream

6. Inflation Hedge: the income stream doesn't grow is the big disadvantage of fixed income investment.

Dividend Growth Investing Strategy

The benefits of a dividend growth investing strategy allow it to be an important a part of portfolio management. Getting paid to await, dividend growth compounding, gaining from bear markets, capital preservation, a frequent income stream, and the opportunity to maintain purchasing power are extremely advantages of dividend growth investing strategies.

Chapter 3 What is DRIP (dividend reinvestment plans)

Dividend Reinvestment Plan (DRIP) is a plan where the dividends that are received automatically reinvest in the underlying stocks/mutual funds/ETFs to acquire more stocks/MFs/ETFs, which in turn will earn more and so on, till the vortex of dividends will set in motion avalanche of cash flow for your whole life.

The dividend is a part of earning income that is distributed to the stakeholders when an organization makes profits. It is important to choose a good solid company that has a wide moat, as Warren Buffet says, at the right price. Dividends reinvesting unleashes the dual force of compounding magic as well as dollar cost averaging, due to the reinvesting of dividends, resulting in a significant accumulation of wealth over a period of time.

DSPP (Direct Stock Purchase Plan):

Direct Stock Purchase Plan (DSPP) is a plan where an investor can purchase the stocks directly from the company without any commissions or fees. These plans are normally handled thru transfer agent who administers them and will charge a very nominal fee. For e.g. Computershare and BNY Mellon manage DRIPs and DSPPs from hundreds of companies, including large and blue chips. DSPP plans allow you to reinvest the dividends, similar to DRIP plans.

Chapter 4   The advantage of DRIP

Dividend reinvestment plan(DRIP) is a cost effective way to put your dividend dollars to worthy use. Instead of spending the dollars or having it sit in a bank account, the money can often buy more stock. Almost all of the programs allow dividends being reinvested for simply no fee. In the rough market, this is a terrific way to buy shares for a lower total price   tag.

Participating in the dividend reinvestment plan forces that you buy stock often. If you're signed up for a DRP, your cash will automatically end up being reinvested. As an end result, with very little effort, you'll adopt a long term horizon for your investments.

Almost all DRIPS carry a solution called optional income purchase. These allow investors to get additional shares for the nominal fee. Many optional cash buy plans have lower minimum investment needs. Some you can spend money on with as low as $10. Maximum investment limits vary based on the plan, though usually that figure reaches to the thousands.

One disadvantage regarding DRIPs is you must keep track of the cost basis on your individual purchases and observe after your own files. If you never, you'll have a lot of work if you ever attempt to sell the stock and must pay tax on your gains.

Chapter 5   How to Retire through Dividend (living off dividends)

The biggest reason anyone wants to get into the world of investing – especially in the dividend sector of the market – is usually so that they can make enough money to cover the expenses that come with retirement. So there's a lot that has to be done to prepare for that day you decide you don't want to do a full 40-hour work week anymore, which starts with deciding which strategy to go with and then then fine tuning it as the market changes over time (because what works now may not work the same way in 20 years).

How to reach those goals is focused on the type of dividend investing that generates a good cash flow for multiple decades, and that's easy done by following these guidelines.

Always Contribute to Your Portfolio

The first rule is in order to continuously add money into your dividend profile, preferably some out of every paycheck or a greater amount every month. What happens is actually that investors are allowed to average the expense of their value over the course of several years.

This provides to be able to build a dividend folder stone by brick of which doesn't require the need to purchase all of your current stock in one single lump sum – which often isn't always the best option for those looking forward to retirement.

If people ignore it, then the benefits are limited as they are only building is already right now there, and even though you will find there's reinvestment option, you'll be able to stand to make all the more money faster with the help of more into your investments. Think about that when you get that third cup of coffee shop brew that you simply average per morning.

Seek Out a Dependable Dividend

The second rule is to maintain a focus on dividend growth stocks, which come from companies that usually offer a consistent raise of rates in distribution to the shareholders. If you want to have your dividend payouts cover your expenses while you are relaxing on the beaches of Maui, then you will want to have a dependable company to invest in for those long periods of time.

That's why investors attempt to find ways to avoid the risk of inflation and put their money in stocks that they can afford to increase their payouts on if they ever need to.

Buy Quality - Not Necessarily Quantity

This task is bringing the savings into a brokerage account pertaining to additional investments, which means a good investor should build a collection of standard screening criteria so that you can have a report on dividend leaders as well as achieves – this is long unless you are able to trim the list to some more manageable amount.

One of what considered is in case a company offers a lot more than 2. 5 per cent, dividends that have observed rises for at the very least 10 years in a row and trading under 20 times already in the market. While some may pun intended, the larger payout ratios – indicative that the company is benefiting a produce spike that won't last for a longer time (you wouldn't much like the dip on this roller coaster) – which could change with respect to the industry the company you happen to be potentially investing falls under.

Quality can become determined after careful research from the details for each stock which helps the investor figure out whether the stock options offers enough to provide a rising revenue rate and correlating dividend obligations over more than just a couple of years, but at least some decades. A properly diversified portfolio will provide good success for the different income stocks which you carefully picked. Speaking of which.

Create a Diversified Portfolio

This is done so that you can not only to lessen the risk of loss, but to shield the investor by means of purchasing stocks from numerous different companies as you can for a far more steady income that will come in during retirement. You don't want to keep all your eggs in 1 basket, as this old saying is going. Some experts consider an investor's stock portfolio should include almost 30 individual companies which are scattered across many industries.

Think of a retail center and the amount of stores one usually has. They don't just have restaurants or department stores. There are specialty stores for gaming fans, photography folks, craftsmen, sports supporters, baby clothes, toys and almost everything in between. Would a mall using 20 or 35 Starbucks sound extremely fun? It likely wouldn't be extremely successful.

Reinvest Wisely

When it comes to putting your money back into your dividend portfolio, don't do it too soon, and let your dividends build up. This is where the power of compounding interest comes into place where you are gaining more money in a shorter time. Not everyone uses that strategy, and most will likely hold their money for safer reinvestments and keep them with the steady growths.

Chapter 6   How to Build a Dividend Portfolio

When it comes to investing in any form of the market, prior knowledge benefits investors the most in their efforts to save for retirement as they work and grow. No one should try to play a sport without having knowledge of the game – otherwise they will not be adequately prepared and will be quickly overtaken by the sharks in the water.

When building a portfolio of dividend stocks, an investor needs to know how to build an income and how it will help cover those financial needs long after you had that retirement celebration at the office where everyone congratulated you for your years of service. This doesn't mean you need to find a get-quick-rich scheme because investing in dividends is something you should plan to have working for you for a few decades – which requires knowing where to start and how to set up a dividend portfolio.

Knowing the Risks of Inflation

Keep in mind that the possibility from the market's risk of inflation – the sustained increase from the prices on goods and services inside economy over a longer time of time – can impact different companies in numerous ways, depending on how much of a direct impact those larger expenses have on exactly where you invest.

There are a variety of risks that have to be kept in mind and weighed against each other when making individuals investment decisions. Experts usually topic themselves to both inflation as well as the market risk concerned, and the amount there're involved varies dependant upon how much thcy diversify their dividend collection. It's a challenging dilemma for everyone who invests while trying to find a dependable income with the long road ahead of time.

For example, a $1 million portfolio with a 5 percent rate usually provides an investor with in relation to $50, 000 on a yearly basis in income that will protect an investor with the aforementioned market possibility. But let's say make fish an inflation rate regarding 3 percent causes the investor to help only have in relation to $35, 000 of getting power about 12 years later. If you put in a tax rate of about 30 percent which $50, 000 then becomes about $25, 000 at the end of 12 years

Benefits of Market Growth

So then, why would you choose to invest in dividends? Just about every portfolio on the market has its own set of risks—even non-guaranteed dividends and other economic risks like the one mentioned a few graphs above where there was a healthy dividend paying list of equities with a 4 percent yield.

Usually these have a payout that increases at least 3 percent each year and covers the inflation rate, possibly growing 5 percent annually over those same 12 years. If the latter were to happen, then that $50,000 you started with would grow to about $90,000 each year, but would be about $62,000 after the planned 3 percent inflation rate. Let's say there is a 15 percent tax (which is always something that can change later on) makes that amount worth about $53,000.

When a portfolio is able to combine both of those methods, it is able to defend itself against the negative effects of inflation and any fluctuations in the stock market. Being able to have a diverse portfolio that includes stocks and bonds is a good way to make a dependable income that won't be affected too much by the potential dividend hazards.

Steps to Building a Dividend Portfolio

1. Create Diversity in Your Portfolio with at least 25 Solid Stock Options

This isn't about trying have King Solomon's gold by starting with nothing. Smart investors remain centered on the long-term goal of experiencing money to fund money during retirement, and that takes time along with patience. Receiving dividends work better focus and besides stock growth and never having to accept a company's possibility.

2. Diversity among Multiple Industries

The right choice means not putting all of your beans in one single pot. For example, if all of your stocks come from different oil companies, it would be a shame if the price per barrel fell as much as $10 or more and would make a negative impact on your dividends. One way of avoiding that dreaded dividend cut is to spread your selections out.

3. Financial Stability is More Important than Growth

Obviously, if the investor had an alternative C for the exam, they might select that you for "both A and B. Which can be a tough thing to try and do, so the 1st priority in the investor is to focus on having far more dependability which means that your company will provide dividends in which increase over time rather than relying upon the prospect of quick growth. This may be accomplished by keeping track of each company you might potentially buy by watching their credit ratings. The Value Line Investment decision Survey commonly grades these types of stocks via A++ and entirely down to the Ds and focus on stocks together with 'A' ratings for your least volume of risk.

4. Look for Companies That Have Modest Payout Ratios

Those ratios are calculated from the dividends as a percentage of the total earnings. If a ratio is 60 percent or less, it means the company has a lot less wiggle room when there could be some unforeseeable trouble down the road. It's best to invest in a company that has a plan for what to do to protect their shareholders in case of any economic crisis.

5. Reinvest What You Earn from Your Dividends

This goes back to the power of compounding that we have talked about in a few of the earlier chapters. By putting the money earned into investments well in advance of when you may need the money for that retirement, the dividends could result in a very surprising amount of growth that doesn't require too much of an effort from the part of the investor.

The Biggest Mistakes to Avoid When Growing Your Portfolio

A big reason why dividends are looking more and more attractive to investors these days is because the yields and bonds are stressfully low, and investors who are looking to plan for their eventual retirement are looking towards dividend-paying stocks for a more dependable income that builds efficiently over a longer period of time.

Dividend investing has become a popular strategy during a time where fixed-income is falling into lows that haven't been hit before and the baby boomer generation is preparing to enter the world of retirement.

That's not to say there isn't any sort of pitfalls, as with anything in the stock market during tough economic times. There are a number of catches in the face of all of the good things that dividend portfolios bring—a list of about seven according to San Francisco advising company, Forward Management, in a report titled How Not to Invest in Dividend Stocks.

Relying on Overly Mechanical Investment Plans

These kinds of strategies often ignore basic shifts as well as dividend policy changes, which could build a problem for the investor's dividend profits flow. This has happened a few times in Europe where many of the telecommunication companies that will paid via benefits had higher makes that had increased beyond completely – which, mentioned previously earlier, is a danger sign that things are planning to go down because what climbs up must come down.

Ignoring a Variety of Growth Factors

Profitable investors have to see and evaluate not only the dividend yields that every company has settled, but also what the company's potential is made for both growth and appreciation – expansion is what allows someone every single child have more settled to them over a longer period of time, which often can help them keep a livable income when they join the old age community.

For illustration, let's imagine that an investor has any portfolio with $1 million and would like to withdraw about $50,000 per annum for expenses like home, food, and so forth. If the trader earns about 3 percent in whole returns, less than 1 / 2 of the starting equilibrium would remain after two decades. Another 10 years later, that same trader earning only 3 percent could well be close to jogging out. Now if in which same person was able to grow their returns to about 7 percentage, they would have savings of about $3 million there after same 30 year period.

Showing Favoritism to the Home Market

There are many options overseas in other countries which have the booming economy that are paying dividends which have higher averages, that are obviously more positive to investors in addition to sometimes provide better options the United states.

Investing in the particular global market has developed into very important factor in the ability to diversify a portfolio by such as industries in those people fast-growing markets. By way of example, people are beginning move cloud surgical procedures overseas to African countries since the demand is increasing there such as Amazon in addition to VMware. In 20 years, those markets get increased their shares in the world economy and are the cause of about 47 percent in the world's gross home product.

Focused Towards Those Blue Chips

Investors sometimes claim there's more safety in having those larger dividend stocks, but they also cost more to buy shares and won't offer as much in return as they once did than the ones that are smaller or middle of the road in cap size. Those larger companies usually offer a liquidity advantage but still don't offer a lot of opportunities to see increased dividend yield.

Investor demand has risen so much that those blue-chip stocks are becoming too costly to even consider as options for a diverse and successful portfolio.

Giving Macro Factors More Weight

There's always about to be plenty of risks with regards to any form regarding investing—it's inevitable as you'll find emerging markets that supply some intriguing probable – especially involving troubled nations along with possible booms in Europe, the Middle East and Africa. Those regions may provide a large number of international revenue benefits and local operations which might be less of times be affected by macro trends.

For example, the stocks from the European market aren't becoming valued as highly due to current crisis which in turn causes doubt for buyers. But there is still a chance to find some stronger companies that offer dividend payments in that part of the world that might provide some potential gains that can help your portfolio.

Chapter 7   How to Rebalance Your Portfolio

Being able to rebalance a dividend portfolio can be an extremely useful way to remove the emotions an investor may have when they make their decisions regarding the ups and the downs of those holdings. Successful investing comes from making smart, diverse decisions that are meant for the long haul, meaning as an investor, you have to be diligent, patient, and willing to stick to your plan rather than look for quick cash.

Establish Your Targets

First, you can start with targets of what is important to like in the dividend portfolio. Having these focused sectors usually works the very best, especially if you're an investor who would like to have up to 30 and up different stocks. While it might be hard to target everyone stock, it's better to spotlight each industry and base your individual decisions on their performance afterwards.

How many you end up picking in each sector is your decision as an entrepreneur – sometimes you need to invest in 10 diverse companies, and sometimes you simply find a couple of. It all is dependent upon how comfortable the investor has been that industry. But concurrently, it's important never to put each of the eggs in 1 basket – you will need a diverse dividend portfolio for top investment success.

One example is, you decide that your particular portfolio will develop the following sectors manifested – financial (15 percent); resources (15); telecommunications (15); power (10); healthcare (10); real estate (10); retail items (10); technology (5); community transport (5); in addition to bonds (5). finance institutions like banks, along with utilities that provide for the public and also telecommunications due to the growing need for mobile technology. The rest are of interest to this hypothetical investor – however while playing it safe given that they feel their bigger cuts develop the best chance to create consistent gains.

Select a Rebalancing Trigger

While some investors use a new once-a-year trigger, many investors usually prefer to see the different stocks into their portfolio more generally than an once-a-year checkup many specialists will recommend one or more times every quarter, if not more. That's because there are so many fees which are linked with buying and selling that you wouldn't want to miss the opportunity to do either along with cost yourself some a lot of money.

Giving yourself about three months to generate a move is generally acceptable because you don't necessarily want to be too hasty in the event that a company which had one minor dip one month could bounce back another. There's an old expression that goes "sell in May and go away" – which is like a warning to sell stocks in the month of May to avoid a potential periodic decline that occurs out there before returning inside the full swing in November when numbers begin to increase again.

Another trigger that lots of investors use is establishing a portion variation for each sector that may decide the rebalancing of one's dividend portfolio. Should your target is to get 10 percent in transportation, you could transfer it 3 percent one of many ways or the other and then, you could decide to sell or buy shares in this sector. The challenge originates from not just modifying one sector but the need to adjust the other six you keep – some experts recommend while using the option to sell with the cash or make investments additional funds.

Take a decision How You Will Rebalance Your Portfolio

Rebalancing a dividend portfolio doesn't mean that the investor has to sell stocks. Sometimes it's just easier to only add funds as a matter of planning how to rebalance the percentages among the sectors in a portfolio.

An investor usually wouldn't sell 10 stocks that are worth $100 and then paying the $10 commission fee because it just doesn't make much sense. Rebalancing your dividend portfolio might not be possible in an efficient manner and requires a large amount of planning before any type of decision is made – remember, working with a dividend investment portfolio means no hasty decisions.

Let's say this hypothetical portfolio, we have mentioned earlier is worth more than $100,000 and most of the investments have at least $5,000. Trades are made worth $1,000 that makes the aforementioned commission fee look really small in comparison – that's considering the 10-20 percent differential target within your portfolio.

Do So within Each Sector

Keep an eye on each of the sectors represented in your dividend portfolio and analyze whether anything needs to be changed internally and not as much on a broad scale. If you own stocks in six banks under the financial sector, there might be an opportunity to rebalance between a few of them based on when you bought the stocks.

Eventually, the stocks that are doing well will need to be sold for a profit that can then be reinvested in the other existing banks in your portfolio. Or you could add a couple of other companies that have shown some great potential for making your portfolio even stronger. Usually when an investor makes this type of decision, they are putting their money in a bank that is providing stronger, more consistent yields as opposed to one in their portfolio that wasn't pulling its weight.

Some experts would recommend waiting until the stock has reached a certain point above the original purchasing price – like around the 20 to 25 percent point. Then an investor is recommended to evaluate the time needed to build that profit and compare it to the other stocks in the portfolio.

Conclusion

I hope this book was able to help you to know about the Dividend Investing.

Finally, if you enjoyed this book, then I'd like to ask you for a favor, would you be kind enough to leave a review for this book on Amazon? It'd be greatly appreciated!

Thank you and good luck!

Book 3

Penny Stocks

A beginner trading guide

By Richard Smiths

Table of Contents

Introduction

Introduction

I want to thank you and congratulate you for downloading the book, Penny stock.

This book contains proven steps and strategies on how to earn in penny stocks.

Everyone wants to achieve financial freedom. People want a life well-lived without having to worry about money. This can actually be achieved but it takes a lot of discipline and focus. A lot of books and articles have been written about different methods to earn money. This book is one of them.

You'll learn a lot of concepts about penny stocks through this book. Although there are some critics to this type of investment, it isn't necessarily bad if you try to learn about it and decide later if you want to dabble in it. What's important is that you have the willingness to learn about penny stocks.

Many think that it's hard to get a job out there in this market, but the truth of the matter is, it's only hard because you're not looking hard enough. I'm writing this book to show you how to use penny stocks, to give you a simple overview on how it's done, why it works, and how to get started in this type of investment that allows you to attain the financial freedom that you need in life.

You will get exact and reliable information in regards to the topic and issue covered. The book is sold with the information that the publisher is not necessary to render accounting, officially acceptable, or otherwise, professional services. If information is necessary, legal or acceptable, an experienced individual in the profession should be ordered.

Thanks again for downloading this book, I hope you enjoy it!

Chapter 1   What is a Penny Stocks?

Penny stocks originate their name from the very low price per share that these stocks are traded.Buyers might sometimes call them "micro-cap stocks," although this type of stock is more often categorized according to market capitalization that falls between $50 and $300 million.

The Securities and Exchange Commission of the United States defines a penny stock as a security that trades at lower than $5 a share. They can be dealt at low prices because these are issued by very small companies and are usually quoted over-the counter (OTC) on Pink Sheets or the OTCBB. However, there are exceptions to the rule such as those traded on securities exchanges. On the contrary, large, publicly traded corporations can command high prices per share and can be found quoted on major stock exchanges.

Generally, a growing company, with limited resources and cash, offers a penny stock to investors. The stock generates low trading volumes because investors don't give it much attention. It is often traded on Pink Sheets and Over-the-counter Bulletin Board. A penny stock is a primary target of market manipulations, which can't be used in stocks traded on the stock market. Therefore, investors must exercise caution when trading penny stocks. It is true that these stocks can generate huge returns but it can also bring about huge losses.

A penny stock has the lowest market capitalization. It is usually subject to adjustment and pump in addition to dump scams. It is furthermore highly volatile and presents a lot of risk to buyers. In the Us, the Economic Sector Monitoring Authority and the SEC have rules and rules for you to define and determine its sale.

Penny trading and investing is not pertaining to small time investors several so-called financial experts recommend. This happens because it involves a good understanding of what sort of market moves. And being unable to tell the signals of when to offer or buy more can be quite frustrating. Fortunately, this book will provide you with insights on tips on how to maximize your endeavor into penny stock investment.

Chapter 2   Find marketplace and brokers

A penny stock broker facilitates trading by offering the necessary trading platform for investors and merchants. He can also influence the buying and selling patterns, preferences, and behaviors on the stakeholders by offering sales, marketing, as well as recommendations. As these kinds of, it is of importance to a trader or investor to find the right broker for his penny stocks investment.

A lots of these brokers currently provide online as well as mobile trading tools. A dematerialized account is a depository of the investor's shares while nostro is the financial institution account for buying and selling shares. Only a few brokers provide nostro features. Since penny trading is highly assuming in nature, price ranges can fluctuate erratically.

Reliable and instant money transfers are needed for timely as well as efficient trading at desired prices. An investor may well suffer significant losses if you'll find bottlenecks in the transfer of cash. Therefore, it 's best for him to select a broker who provides both nostro as well as depository facilities.

When it comes to penny stocks, transactional costs play an important role. It is important for the investor to learn about transaction prices, which can easily be located on the broker's website. The individual must also take particular discover of additional fine print listed on the website.

Some brokers may charge the very least brokerage fee every share. This signifies that an additional fee per share could possibly be charged to the investor for each and every transaction. For example, a $0. 10 inventory with $0. 03 minimum broker agent fee per share will surely cost about $0. 13 every share. For 10, 000 shares of an penny stock, the investor should pay $300 a lot more than the present market price.

Some brokers can also charge a bare minimum brokerage fee every order. For example, a 1, 000 shares involving penny stock with economy price of $0. 01 and 3% broker agent or $10 bare minimum brokerage fee every trade order will surely cost the investor $10. 30. However, since $0. 30 is lower than $10, the investor should pay the $10 bare minimum brokerage fee. Thus, he will pay $20 for your transaction.

A broker can also set additional prices for large purchases. This large order surcharge will apply in the event the investor buys shares that happen to be more than the maximum shares set because of the broker.Also the broker can also set monthly bare minimum trades. If an investor doesn't meet the required amount of trades, he could possibly be charged an additional fee.

There can also be an annual preservation fee, which is billed by brokers for each and every trading account. Additional charges can also include fees for cash transfers, depository records, etc. Some brokers also demand a minimum deposit to open a penny stock trading bill. Furthermore, they also fee additional fees for accounts which have been inactive for an extended time. They may also charge a withdrawal fee each time money is transferred in the trading account to the investor's bank.

Now that you might have the basics down and you are mentally prepared to purchase penny stocks, it's time to find where these are listed. The key stock exchanges such as NASDAQ and NYSE accomplish list cheap stocks, but these will not be necessarily considered penny stocks. As previous, these exchanges possess stringent requirements of which companies must fulfill and companies trading penny stocks are simply not around their standards nevertheless. So, penny stocks are traded such as off-exchange, it means that they're dealt without assistance from a stock exchange. Unlike exchange buying and selling, the market prices will not be published and remain involving the two parties engaged inside transaction. This boosts the risks involved in trading.

OTC Markets Class, also known because Pink Sheets, is a listing service that provides market information for OTC securities. Listed companies will not be registered with the SEC and have no minimum needs for trading. The OTC Message Board (OTCBB) can also be used for NON-PRESCRIPTION securities. It offers more transparency in comparison with Pink Sheets, but market capitalization as well as minimum share price will not be required. Companies previously stated on stock exchanges but forget to sustain requirements would often turn out trading on OTCBB.

The best way to trade penny stocks is with an online dealer. It would be good to select brokers who specialize in penny stocks. Take notice that different traders defined a penny stocks differently. Pick brokers who charge a set rate in relation to trade commissions. The reason being the volume is important when trading penny stocks and you don't want to increasingly save money to raise your financial well being. A per-share agreement becomes very limiting over time. Also, be wary of any fees how the broker will fee and for whichever reasons. You are able to trade an unlimited amount of shares without having to pay extra. Understand any different special terms how the broker imposes in clients so you don't get surprised simply by rules and limits.

As with every other business, customer services important. Friendly, thorough and easily accessible support can make yourself easier you probably have any issues or inquiries. Some brokers may also be more generous than others in relation to sharing market data and research. A broker who sends alerts for stocks to exchange would be very useful in helping you navigate the market.

Some brokers have a tendency to limit choices according to the price per write about or other attributes. Their digital trading platform should have an easy-to-navigate user interface that you can understand. Find out if they have support for all you devices such while laptops, tablets and smartphones and your OS of choice as well as other system requirements.

As a result of price volatility of penny stocks, the hold time on the phone and the response time on the website are prime considerations. An investor has to enter or depart a position instantly because prices can change quickly. If they needs different purchaser services like stories and research tools, technical indicators, as well as data feeds, it is vital that he consult his broker regarding their costs because most of these services are offered for a high fee.

How to invest in penny stocks

Open up a Trading Bank account

When an entrepreneur opens a buying and selling account, he must consider support services, fees, and how quickly funds is usually transferred. There are stockbrokers with various specializations so it will be best for him to buy around for a free account which matches their requirements.

A penny stock investor should be very concerned in regards to the broker's fee construction. There are stockbrokers who charge profits per share, that is a scheme with a set rate for the very least number of shares. They also fee another rate for succeeding shares. This fee structure is designed for an investor who has low capital. Regarding penny stock merchants, it is more cost-effective to search for a broker who gives a low flat pace per transaction. Having a low fee, the trader can generate a higher price because of much less commissions and costs.

Chapter 3   How to Choose the Right Penny Stock

Not all stocks listed about the OTCBB will get listed into a major stock trade. Most companies will likely be bankrupt or fade into oblivion also before they benefit from their products and services. However, the trading volume of OTCBB still remains its phenomenal progress. About 650 billion shares happen to be traded in 2006. majority penny stock companies haven't any revenue. However, it is easy for traders to be able to choose a company which will probably succeed.

The first place where one can look into when judging the soundness of purchasing a penny stock would be the financial statements from the company. Seeing high debt and low sales just isn't necessarily a red flag because a lot of startup companies do begin the life cycle this method. Losses are expected at the start with positive income finally coming in perhaps by another financial year. These businesses are not instantly busts. Take a peek at the business that the company is operating in. Is it an emerging specialized niche? Does the item have promise in the years to come? Do your research and find out what the experts assert about the companies engaged inside a similar area. In recent many years, tech startups have become a dime a dozen. But, there are those that really offer revolutionary I. T. remedies that consumers react positively to. Often, a product may be quite in advance of its time similar to the predecessor of this Apple MacBook laptop computers. The big, clunky laptops were fun and stylish, but during the time, people were still observing their way around desktop PCs. A few decades after, MacBook have become the benchmark inside laptop design and quality. Learn to realize potential before all others does.

Also, keep abreast associated with rumors of mergers and acquisitions that smaller companies are inclined to. These usually create a beneficial rise inside stock prices, especially if at all the latter. Either way, the news will create interest in the stocks, so you'll want to monitor any developments so you will know how to proceed with the stocks that you're holding. Young companies at the start of their life cycle is definitely the ones that would experience sudden growths. This tapers away or plateaus since the company matures and stock prices stabilize. Thus, the beginning is an excellent time to start buying the company. You can find that penny stocks could multiply in value in a mere a matter associated with hours. Understand in which the company is inside its life never-ending cycle. If it already quite after dark infancy stage but still has very reduced share prices, then there can be something inherently wrong with all the way it is progressing business and you ought to no longer be waiting for some time when the stocks would suddenly rise in value.

Creating Probability Work

A penny stock investor must know what sort of company he's seeking. In addition, he must also possess the appropriate tools to assist him look to find the best stock. Since the average price of a cent stock is $0. 10, will probably be best to seek out stocks priced involving $0. 05 and $2. If the investor wants to search for a higher-priced any amount of money stock, he could find fewer stocks.

He must seek out penny stocks with at the very least 100, 000 stocks of average everyday volume. The focus have to be on those stocks which are on an uptrend. Thus, the trader can use the positive 3-week and 10-week price information, and with this 9-day simple moving average in excess of its 18-day opposite number. The trader can easily exclude companies having negative earnings progress rates or damaging earnings per discuss. He must concentrate on stocks on a good uptrend for at the very least a 5-day time period. He must be thinking about stocks which are often on an uptrend.

Each penny stock must pass what is this great, short interest, and visual tests. A wholesome chart pattern becomes necessary. It must show that the price is when using uptrend and going above the assist levels. To pass what is this great test, the penny stock company must create positive news so as to attract more traders. A short interest is often a percentage of the whole shares which was sold short yet hadn't been closed yet. If this percentage is higher than 5%, it can mean trouble. However, if this percentage continues to increase, it will push the cost even higher.

Selecting the Winners

A retail trader may commit one of his biggest exchanging mistakes if he sees a cent stock as something is affordable. He believes that he will bring in more cash if he tends to buy more shares of one penny stock as an alternative to buying shares of the higher-priced stock listed on a major exchange. Although it may look rational, it is important that he doesn't overlook the number of shares outstanding.

For instance, companies A and B have $100, 000, 000 industry capitalization each. Should the share price associated with company A can be $0. 10, it indicates that its amount of shares outstanding is add up to 1, 000, 000, 000. In contrast, if company B's discuss price is $100, its amount of shares outstanding can be 1, 000, 000. Thus, before company Some sort of gets fully capitalized, it requires investors to purchase the 1, 000, 000, 000 stocks. It is simpler to sell 1, 000, 000 stocks at $100 as compared to 1, 000, 000, 000 stocks at $0. 10.

An investor must also be familiar with dilution of penny stocks. This means a stock's number associated with shares outstanding may grow uncontrollable by using employee investment, stock splits, and share issuance to improve capitalization. If the business issues more stocks, ownership percentage of investors will likely be diluted. Therefore, if an investor wants to achieve success in penny stocks, he must have the ability to search for a company that includes a very strong share structure making sure that existing owners won't view the value of their own investment eroded through continuous dilution

Spotting the most beneficial Penny Stock

Cent stock companies include low market capitalization. Everyone, who wants to invest in them, must take into account the fundamentals of these firms. He must find out about their share composition, competition, and underlying fundamentals making sure that he'll have the ability to determine the most effective stock to invest in.

The investor should also know the areas where these penny stocks belong. Most penny stocks are in this mining and alloys sector. Aggressive inducement plans, increased opposition, and fund operations have to be considered if he wants to earn more revenue from these penny stocks.

Using Financial Ratios to determine the Winning Stock

If a any amount of money stock company has the capacity to provide adequate monetary disclosure, the investor are capable of doing analysis to determine if at all worth investing in it. If there's having a positive trend and strong numbers about the financial statements, he will be able to foretell the future expectations of performance from the penny stock business.

The Liquidity ratios

These ratios are widely-used to compute for penny stocks since many are unable to afford their short-term debt. If the liquidity relation is low, it indicates that the any amount of money stock company can be advancing its procedures or struggling to remain in business.

The particular Leverage Ratios

Leverage ratios resemble liquidity ratios. Both of them concentrate on the ability from the penny stock company to its debts. Nevertheless, with leverage ratios, the concern can be on long-term credit card debt.

The Performance Percentage

The performance relation quantifies the revenues generated by the company through the income statement. It's important for a any amount of money stock company showing consistent earnings progress.

The Valuation Ratios

Valuation ratios measure the penny stock's attractiveness at its existing price. In common, it is easy for a penny stock to become significantly overvalued. An investor can use these ratios as tools to determine if a certain stock is overvalued or even undervalued.

Chapter 4   Advice for Penny Stock Trading

Penny stocks are very susceptible to fraud and hoaxes. Trading penny stocks is definitely not for the actual faint of heart. The high risks that come with very volatile stocks might cause many less seasoned traders to forfeit their cool and panic once values commence to plummet. But, that is the nature of penny stocks. As with any other kind of stock, time should be working for you. Patience is key to investing. Here you can easily see some advice for you if you wish to start penny trading.

Learn to recognize the real superstars among the actual wannabes. Do not get attached to any one company for sentimental (It was my first deal!), emotional (It is run by way of nice old n lady!) or maybe truly irrational (I like their gooseberry jam that nobody different likes!) reason. Drop the within performing stocks if it is time and keep the good ones providing it still makes sense for this. Always have the mindset of a businessman who can abandon a settling ship when it becomes sure it will only bring about more losses. Remember that you have no obligation to be faithful to a new company's stock, no matter the amount personal or relational investment you may have with it. Your financial investment must always reign supreme.

Follow the best rule of financial, which is diversification. Simply put: usually do not put all your eggs in a single basket. When a single spoils, it affects the others and you lose all of your eggs. Thus, place your money in various kinds of investments instead of placing all of your money in just one. Do not hope that one company's penny stocks is likely to make you rich. That may be increasing risk in an already risky circumstance. Likewise, do not only invest in penny stocks, but also recognize less volatile blue penny stocks coming from large corporations using a long history connected with excellent business performance and good predictions. Furthermore, do not only invest in stocks and options, but also consider bonds, real house, and even gold bars. Investing in penny stocks take a great deal of commitment because these people move so rapidly. Daily monitoring of your stocks is critical. Letting your stocks sit for an extended time without trading is just not ideal. Learn to adapt to changing market environments to maximize your earnings.

Monitor the price Up and down of Some Penny Stocks

Because a trader can buy a sizable volume of shares, he can crank out large profits if you take advantages of every day changes in the price of the penny stock. In addition, by using short-term strategies, the investor has to cope with lesser risks.

Avoid the Hype
A lot connected with penny stock companies are doing artificial methods to increase the

value of their stock by enticing inexperienced investor to purchase them by buying shares of stock. Because more buyers are receiving into the penny stock, it is actually expected that it is price will substantially increase. This is rooked by unscrupulous folks and businesses by selling their particular shares for a higher price. Thus, traders really should make a thorough research firstly the business before buying it. The historical price fluctuations is usually analyzed and economic news works extremely well in order to gauge when the penny stock is a superb investment or not.

Use Effective Techniques

To maximize gains and mitigate risk, an individual can certainly trade consistently just one stock and remember to research about the actual company's business. He can learn quickly and with assurance predict any transform in value by using effective strategies. A lot of penny stock companies have small-scale businesses and generate lower revenues monthly. These enterprises can easily collapse. As this kind of, it is better to select a penny stock company using a broad customer base. The investor can also choose a company which is in to high-demand product or service and service growth.

Analyze Volume

In choosing the penny stock, the trader must pick a business which offers high amount of shares. Top penny stocks work extremely well for day buying and selling activities if these types of stocks have 1000 of shares at a low price. The person can purchase and sell these stocks often for short amounts of time in order to be able to earn more gains. However, it's important to discover if there is a lot of investors and traders who definitely are interested in buying and selling the shares of this company. If we have a high demand to get a particular penny stock, the shares can certainly generate substantial gains. By analyzing the actual trading volume, a trader can pick the right penny stocks for his day trading investing strategies.

Take Benefit of Volatility

A lot of investors can preserve shares of stock for so many years before locking of their profits by selling them. Within this long time frame, the company sells all its assets, be merged having another company, or go out of business. On another hand, top penny stocks, which are additional volatile, can be ordered by traders and sold before the trading day finishes. The volatility of penny stocks ensures that the actual traders sell their shares inside day so that you can maximize the short-term gains.

Buy The Shares Of Stock At The Appropriate Time

If there's a new sharp drop inside value of a penny stock, a lot connected with its shareholders will want to sell their explains to you. Therefore, a large amount of the stock is available for purchase at a good deal. Once the explains to you are bought, it really is imperative for the actual trader to keep track of the fluctuations of the price until this tops its typical daily peak next the shares can always be sold for greatest profit.

Chapter 5 Why Investors Need To Be Worried

A penny stock, especially one that trades below $0. 01, is usually thinly traded.

Manipulators and stock promoters often utilize it for its water pump and dump structure. They initially buy the majority of this stock after that inflate its talk about price through misleading and false claims.

A pump along with dump scheme is fraudulent. Some organizations or individuals invest in penny stock explains to you and use mail blasts, fake pr releases, stock message snowboards, chat rooms, and websites to build interest to your stock. In most cases, a person will claim undertake a hot tip about a particular penny stock so that you can persuade naive investors to acquire the shares swiftly. When more investors find the shares, the price will skyrocket to entice more investors to purchase the shares. Finally, the manipulators will sell there shares and generate huge profits there.

For example, rapper 50 Dollar used Twitter to help dramatically increase the price tag on HNHI, a penny stock. He owned thirty million shares and was able to earn $8. 7 million through the sale. Another example could be the case of Lithium Seek Group whose current market capitalization went approximately at least $350 million following company executed a comprehensive mail campaign. In the 10-Q form the organization filed on December 31, 2010, it listed the firm with no assets and absolutely nothing revenues. After your promotion, it bought lithium exploration properties to cope with the concerns of the press.

In a number of cases, a company are capable of doing a pump along with dump when it desires to promote its stock. In general, the price tag on the penny stock moves because of momentum. It is volatile with the spread and the way the Securities and Exchange Commission regulates the idea. The SEC can halt the exchanging when it updates that its price went up very rapid. Until such time that it is released by SECURITIES AND EXCHANGE COMMISSION'S again, the price of the penny can move either way and investors don't have got control over their shares.

Regulating the Trade of penny stocks

In the United states of America, a penny stock must meet different standards like minimum shareholder equity, current market capitalization, and price tag. A publicly-listed stock, which is dealt around the stock exchange, just isn't controlled like a penny stock even although its price is below $5. It really is classified as some sort of low-priced stock and not as a any penny stock. The Financial Marketplace Regulatory Authority and also the Securities and Exchange Commission control penny stock trading through their rules and regulations. The State regarding Georgia was the very first to enact a wide penny stock legislation. After the legislation was upheld by the US District The courtroom, the SEC and also the FINRA made comprehensive revisions on their regulations, which had been effective in confining or closing traders and brokers. Even so, pump and dispose of schemes by unregistered individuals and groups never have been addressed by simply these regulations.

Understanding the Risk

A penny stock can be quite volatile. Putting money from it may result to help substantial gains but we have a greater probability of experiencing losses. As this sort of, it is important for any investor to watch out for trading penny futures. Money managers, common funds, and index finances have set rules to visit so they can't trade penny stocks. Therefore, only several investors place their money in penny stocks. It is important to note that the issue of liquidity can't end up being ignored. A retail investor may get stuck with a penny stock for an extended time if there is not enough supply and demand for him to trade   his   stock.

Chapter 6   The Risks and Potential

Investing penny stocks can be be extremely risky but it also has a great potential to get significant returns. On the other hand, it must be noted large amounts of people gamble on penny stocks and significant returns could be generated over the short term. A lot connected with companies offering penny stocks are usually more than leveraged or headed towards bankruptcy. Some corporations are furthermore shell companies that scammers use to dupe people.

The Risks Of Penny stocks Trading

In nearly all cases, penny stocks are traded on Over-the-counter Bulletin Table or Pink Bed sheets. An investor will find challenging looking for information about companies offering their stocks around the OTCBB so he will find it hard to make a logical conclusion of a particular company. Additionally, for both Pink Sheets and OTCBB, we have a lack of trustworthy sources about these stocks. In simple fact, listing on sometimes exchange doesn't even call for a company to fulfill some minimum expectations.

Furthermore, there is a lot of liquidity in trading penny stocks. It may be possible to get a penny stock but disposing the actual shares will pose a problem because the trading volume can be quite low. This means the investor will find it hard to sell his penny stock even when he wants to lock in his profits because you will discover fewer interested buyers on the target price. The investor will likely then have to watch for a willing customer or sell the stock at the lower price. When the person decides to wait, he may find himself trapped in a very pump-and dump plan and sees even his capital being erased. If he decides to reduce the price, he will see a reduction in his profits.

Finally, there are a great number of scammers offering biased tips about a particular penny stock. A likely investor may obtain brochures through electronic mail or snail postal mail. The material, usually contains a number of hyped-up claims the specific penny inventory will experience significant gains as a result of revolutionary technology. The unsuspecting individual doesn't understand that the person or even company sending the brochures is selling his individual shares at discounted prices.

Penny Stock Scams

A penny Stock can pose problems not simply to the individual, but to the actual Securities and Exchange Commission likewise. Its poor liquidity and lack of information make it a simple target for scammers.

Some penny Stock companies pay individuals to recommend the actual stock using several media like radio stations shows, newsletters, and also financial television. An investor may be given a spam email informing him of an great earning chance. It is best for your person to check should the people recommending the stock are being paid for his or her services.

It is usually possible for an investor to be scammed by offshore brokers. The SEC allows companies to sell stocks to overseas investors offshore with no need to register the actual stocks. What these businesses do is which they sell their explains to you of stock at the discount to overseas buyers, who then sell them returning to investors in the United states of America at the higher price. These offshore brokerages often make cold calls to potential investors and give hot tips to entice those to buy the inventory.

Avoid Getting scammed

Most penny stock companies advertise through e-mail spam. Similar to spam, these emails contain success stories of which purport " I managed to get $1, 000 richer everyday! " and stories that confess " My spouse and i was skeptical in the beginning, but I feel now a believer throughout Company X!. Penny stocks should be consumed seriously. It isn't as simple as choosing a magic bean and also watching it grow right beanstalk that contains money

Jordan Belfort with the Wolf of Walls Street fame after said about options trading, " As long as it gets done, the item doesn't matter just how. " Lying, cheating and crime are typical fair game to be able to brokers and companies that are set on making bank on the expense of naive investors. A common myth that is spread to likely investors is of which Walmart stocks was previously penny stocks. That is untrue. The source of the misunderstanding is based on their split-adjusted price during which adjustments were done for their historic stock prices despite the fact that they were by no means traded at any amount of money stock prices. Walmart did start off trading OTC for a couple years just before being eventually listed around the NYSE. A identical story has spread about Microsoft, but stock splits are once again the reason for the sub-$1 costs.

When doing pursuit, it is sometimes better to disregard any information willingly provided by management. They will declare and do anything that you buy their stocks. They will help to make false promises and also downplay existing issues within their organizations. It is the most suitable to do your own personal independent research or count on information provided by credible vacation sources. Also, steer clear of promotional resources, press releases along with other media and promoting presence, because they come directly through the companies themselves and can easily be misrepresented.

Finally, never pay for information. Find bloggers whom give advice and tricks for free to his or her readers. Join online groups that discuss very cheap stocks and provide you with up-to date news around the markets. Books, fund journals, newspapers and periodicals should publish additional legitimate information rather than online sources that not go through editorial reviews or even expert criticism.

Buying stocks is any high-stakes game, but this is a game that ought to be played strategically along with the proper way of thinking lest one declines victim to dishonest those who only want to exploit people who are blinded with the promise of easy money through penny stocks.

Why Is A Penny Stock A Risky Investment?

First, the public doesn't have a access to just about all information. To be successful in investing, an investor need to have enough tangible information to assist him make a fantastic decision. Those companies listed on Pink Linens don't file with SEC in order that they aren't regulated or perhaps scrutinized publicly. Moreover, more information about they then isn't credible.

Next, Pink Sheets along with Over-the-counter Bulletin Table don't require companies to fulfill some minimum standard requirements. It may be possible for a company to become listed on these exchanges since it failed to keep its position about the major exchange. The OTCBB calls for listed companies to at the very least file SEC documents regularly. However, Pink Linens doesn't have just about any requirement.

Third, the majority of listed companies within OTCBB and Pink Sheets are both nearing bankruptcy or perhaps newly created. Thus, these companies could possibly have no track record by any means. It is very difficult to determine the potential of anything stock if the company doesn't have famous information.

Fourth, penny stocks have liquidity issues. It is possible that the investor won't be able to dispose his stock options because he can't find a willing buyer correctly. He may even have to lower his cost if he desires to sell it quickly. Furthermore, some unscrupulous men and women and companies may manipulate the price of a penny stock options through pump along with dump scheme.

This Potential Of Penny Stock

To make money with penny stocks, an individual must get along with the pump-and get rid of scheme. This means which he buys the stock options when he will get the spam email or spam then wait with the other people to purchase it also in order that the trading volume is going to be increased. However, the investor should sell his stocks quickly to freeze his small gains. Timing is crucial with such a strategy. If he misses your initial surge in exchanging volume, he may eventually lose just about all his capital.

Another strategy is to list all penny stocks and perform required research on companies that are fitted with generated revenues, made available liquid stocks, and operated the best website with firm images and get in touch with information. In supplement, these companies need to have a strong stability sheet or is actually debt-free, and include reduced losses or perhaps remained profitable

The Fallacy On the Penny Stock

Unsuspecting investors are made to believe that a lot of currently popular stocks began as penny stock. They believed in which today's large businesses only appreciated within values. By performing required research, an investor will be aware that companies like Wal-Mart and Microsoft had been reduced to pennies as a consequence of stock splits. They then didn't start their businesses at the low market cost.

Lastly, a lot of investors become attracted to penny stocks since they believe that these kinds of stocks will appreciate and give more opportunities. For instance, a $0. 10 reveal price, which likes to $0. 15, has made a 50% earnings. Therefore, a $1, 000 investment has the capacity to buy 10, 000 shares along with earns $500 after the increase in price. Investors fail to realize that if it's probable to earn $500 from your transaction, it is also possible to reduce $500 or the many capital.

Conclusion

Thank you again for buying this book!

I hope this book was able to help you to understand and get started on trading penny stocks.

Finally, if you enjoyed this book, then I'd like to ask you for a favor, would you be kind enough to leave a review for this book on Amazon? It'd be greatly appreciated!

Thank you and good luck!

www.ingramcontent.com/pod-product-compliance
Lightning Source LLC
Chambersburg PA
CBHW071819200526
45169CB00018B/437